The Book of Turtles

Sy Montgomery & Matt Patterson

Bog Turtle

Clarion Books

An Imprint of HarperCollins*Publishers*

To Ann and David Patterson,
with gratitude

Clarion Books is an imprint of HarperCollins Publishers.

The Book of Turtles

ISBN 978-0-35-845807-4

The illustrations in this book were done with acrylic paint.
Many depict individual turtles the artist has personally known.
Typography by Phil Caminiti
23 24 25 26 27 PC 10 9 8 7 6 5 4 3

First Edition

Sometime around 240 million years ago—about the time of the first dinosaurs, and 9 million years before the first crocodile—the shell invented the turtle.

Pascagoula Map Turtle

A turtle's shell is composed of 60 joined bones, including ribs and spinal column, all covered by keratin, the stuff of our fingernails.
The shell makes a turtle a turtle.

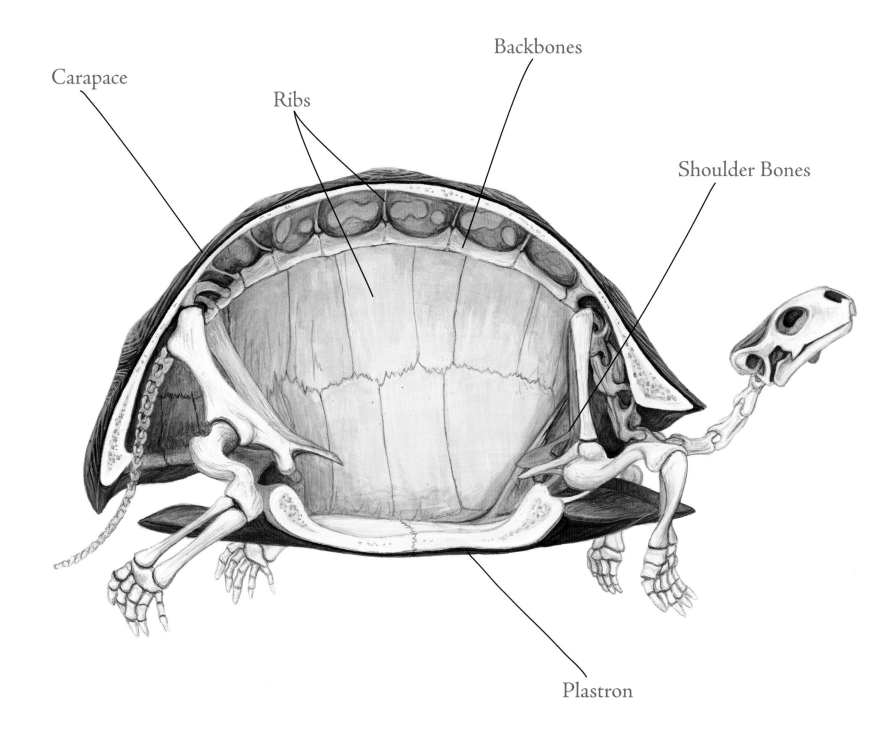

Backbones

Carapace

Ribs

Shoulder Bones

Plastron

Like lizards, snakes, and crocodiles, turtles are reptiles. All reptiles use the sun's warmth to heat their bodies, sport scaly skin, and lay eggs on land. But only turtles have the wonderful shell.

The shell is one reason why turtles can live so long: protected by such effective armor, some species can live for two centuries. The shell permits a slow pace—no need to hurry when you're safe.

Radiated Tortoise

The turtle shell began from the bottom up.

The turtle's oldest known ancestor, a fossil reptile discovered in Germany in 2015, looked like a lizard with a hard belly shield, protecting it from predators swimming up from below. Scientists named the fossil *Pappochelys*—"Grandfather of Turtles." To guard against predators coming from above, the top shell developed millions of years later. By 220 million years ago, turtles that look much like today's flourished right alongside the dinosaurs.

The top of the shell
is called the carapace.

The bottom of the shell
is called the plastron.

Wood Turtle

The top and bottom are connected with bony parts called bridges. Some turtles can pull their heads, feet, and tails inside their shells to protect them. Some just tuck their necks to the side. A few have heads so big they can't retract them into the shell at all.

Because it's part of the turtle's skeleton, a turtle can't leave its shell—no more than you can walk off and leave your bones behind.

But there's a lot more to love about turtles than their amazing shells. We love their slowness— a balm amid a world filled with human hurry. We love that turtles can live so long. One had a baby at age 140. Another died at age 288. He was alive when George Washington was born!

Aldabra Giant Tortoise

More than 300 different kinds of turtles grace our planet. The turtles that lumber about on thick, column-like legs on land are called tortoises.

Spider Tortoise

Seven species of sea turtles spend almost all their lives
swimming in the ocean. (The females return to land to lay eggs.)

Kemp's Ridley Sea Turtle

Turtles that live in brackish water, where a river meets the sea, are sometimes
called terrapins. (The word was taken from the Algonquian language of the
Native people of New England.) All of them are turtles.

Diamondback Terrapin

Turtles come in startling colors. Some are red. Some are yellow. Some change color. The male northern river terrapin, native to Asia, changes the color of his head from olive brown to ebony, and his neck and forelegs to crimson, to attract a female. Even his irises change color, from black to yellow-white. In 2015, scientists discovered that the Hawaiian hawksbill turtle's shell and body glow in the dark of night: red, green, and yellow. We don't yet know why.

Northern River Terrapin

There are turtles with soft shells; turtles with googly eyes; turtles with necks longer than their bodies; and turtles with giant heads and grasping tails.

Because of the shell, everyone can recognize a turtle. But turtles surprise us.

Big-headed Turtle

Black-breasted Leaf Turtle

Malayan Softshell Turtle

Extreme Turtles

Largest: Leatherback Sea Turtle. Its teardrop-shaped shell can stretch seven feet long. Leatherbacks can weigh more than 2,000 pounds—one ton (almost as much as a small car)—making it the fourth-heaviest species of reptile alive today. Only three species of crocodiles weigh more.

Smallest: Speckled Padloper Tortoise. Males grow only three inches long; females grow to nearly four inches. It's native to Namibia and western South Africa.

Actual size!

Fastest: Spiny Softshell Turtle. This large North American turtle can sprint faster than 15 miles per hour—faster than the average 10-year-old doing the 100-meter dash—and swims faster yet. Unlike most turtles, its shell feels rubbery because it is covered with soft skin.

Flattest: Pancake Tortoise. A thin, flat, flexible shell helps this turtle escape predators by allowing it to squeeze into gaps between rock crevices in its arid home in Kenya and Tanzania.

Longest Necks (relative to body): Snake-necked Turtles. This group of related species, native to Australasia and South America, got their name because they look like someone tried to stuff a snake into a turtle shell. In some species, the head and neck can stretch for 10 inches—longer than the length of the carapace.

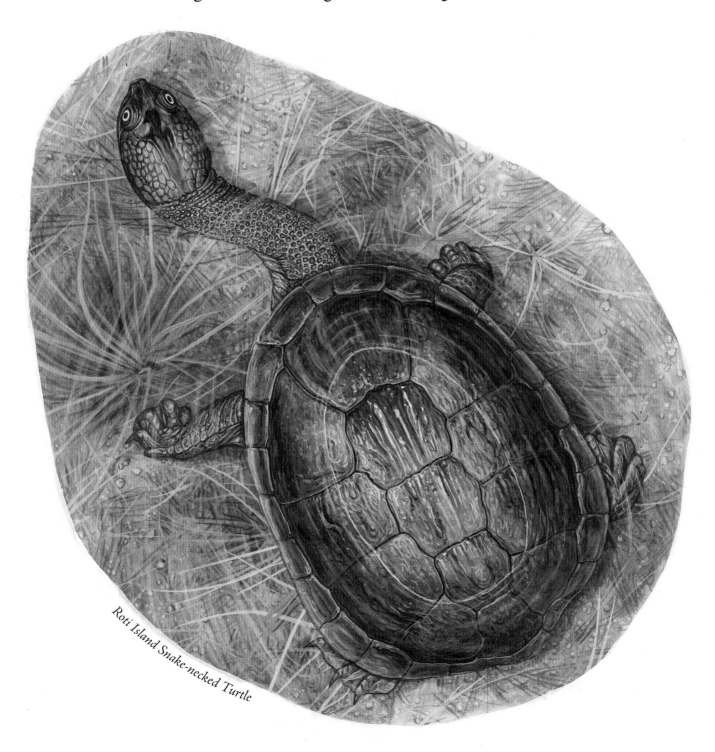

Roti Island Snake-necked Turtle

Most Colorful: Western Painted Turtle.
This eye-catching subspecies lives in ponds from
western Ontario and British Columbia south into
the central United States. You can often
see these turtles basking on logs
on sunny summer days.

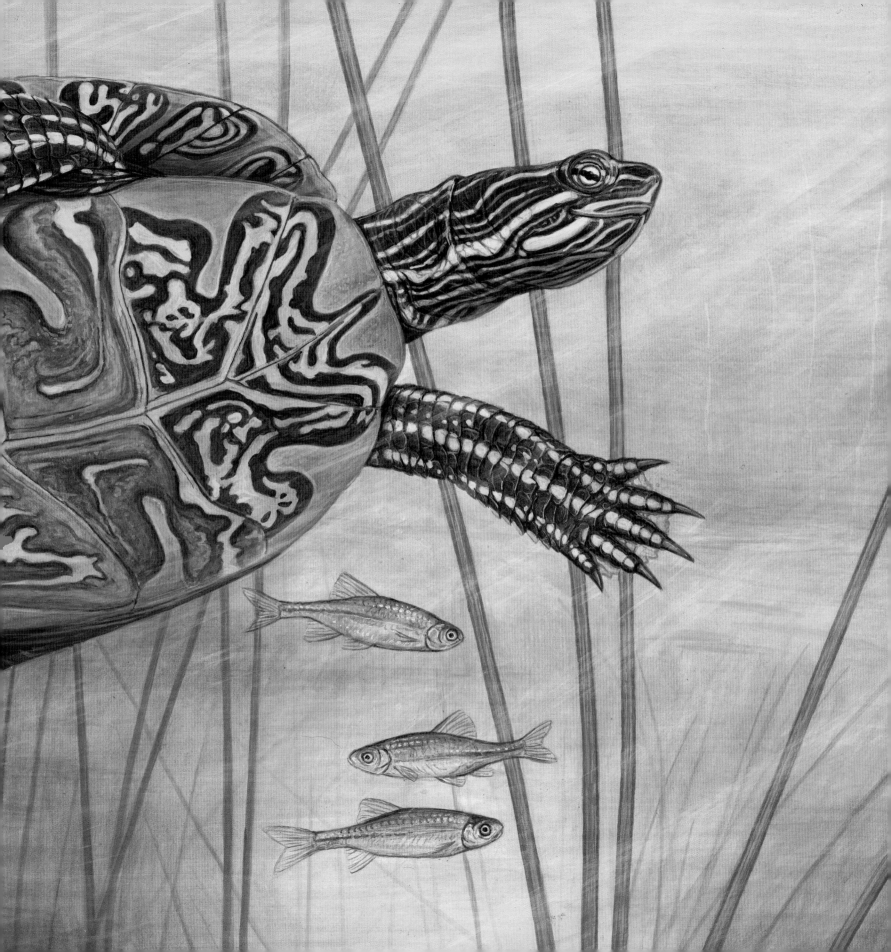

Stinkiest: African Helmeted Turtle. When disturbed or threatened, it emits a foul-smelling musk from glands under each leg. This species smells even worse than eastern North America's famously named stinkpot turtle, which releases its stench from glands at the edge of its shell.

Longest Life Span:

Aldabra Giant Tortoise. Several individuals of this species, native to the island nation of Seychelles in the Indian Ocean, are reported to have lived to more than 250 years.

Turtles' many talents astound.

Turtles are surprisingly smart. Wood turtles can learn a maze as quickly as laboratory rats. Even old turtles can learn new tricks. A 90-year-old green sea turtle named Myrtle quickly mastered a complex task that involved three platforms, two boxes with speakers, and one box with a light. If the light went on in the light box, she was to touch that platform with her flipper for a food reward. But if the light went on while a tone was playing from one of the other boxes, she had to decide which speaker was making the sound and touch that platform instead.

Some turtles even hunt. The African helmeted turtle sometimes hunts in packs, seizing ducklings from below, or drowning doves as they come to drink. They also eat ticks and biting flies off rhinos and hippos—which is why the big mammals seek out wallowing holes hosting these turtles for a spa treatment.

Though turtles are famously slow, some are adept athletes. Many turtles climb. An eastern box turtle can scale a chain-link fence. The Asian big-headed turtle climbs branches and shrubs to cross over streams.

Eastern Box Turtles

Some female turtles store sperm—sometimes for years. Since most turtles are solitary, there are limited chances to meet a mate. Mating can't always be timed so that eggs are ready to lay when conditions are right. One female box turtle waited 10 years to lay fertile eggs after her last meeting with a male.

Some turtles, including the eastern painted turtle, can lie buried in cold water for months on end in the winter. How do they survive?

They breathe through their bottoms. The cloaca—the single hole through which a turtle poops, pees, mates, and lays eggs—features two sacs, called bursa, filled with blood vessels that efficiently absorb oxygen during hibernation.

Other turtles tinkle through their mouths. The Chinese softshell terrapin immerses its head in a puddle. It sucks, swills, and spits out water for up to 100 minutes—while tiny structures inside its mouth flush out urea, the waste product in urine. In this turtle's brackish water home, this system works 15–50 times better than kidneys.

And that's not all!
In addition to being clever, some turtles can even be deceptive.

The matamata, a freshwater turtle in South America, looks like a decaying leaf.

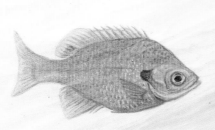

The alligator snapper has a lure in the mouth which looks like a yummy, pink worm.

The four-eyed turtle looks like it has six eyes. The biggest eyes aren't eyes at all, but spots on the top of the head. The spots fool predators into thinking it's a much larger animal that has already seen them.

You can't see any ears on a turtle. But they're not deaf. They have a disk membrane in back of the face, giving them a larger range of hearing than any other reptile. They can hear you whisper. Many turtles can also detect sounds too low for human ears to register. They need to listen because . . .

Red-footed Tortoise

... turtles talk.

At least eight species of giant South American river turtles communicate underwater with low-pitched calls to help them travel together and find mates—and maybe more. We are still learning turtles' secrets!

Travancore tortoises chorus at night. Each voice is different. Nobody knows why they call.

A frightened giant musk turtle yelps like a dog. The southern Vietnam box turtle whistles.

Leatherback mothers belch when they're nesting, and the babies begin to call to each other, in voices too low for humans to hear, while still inside the egg. This helps the babies hatch and dig out of the nest at the same time, when it's less likely that one predator could eat them all.

Male tortoises grunt, groan, cluck, and shout. (In the movie *Jurassic Park*, one of the sounds the velociraptors make is actually a soundtrack of tortoises mating.)

Southern Vietnam Box Turtle

South American River Turtles

Turtles are individuals with distinct personalities.

Some are bold. Some are shy. Some love their necks rubbed, while others like their shells scratched.

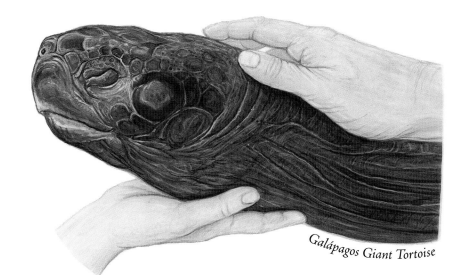

Galápagos Giant Tortoise

African Spur-thigh Tortoise

Most prefer that people leave them alone. Turtles, like people, have thoughts and feelings. Each turtle is different from all the others.

Celebrity Turtle Profiles

Lonesome George was a male Pinta Island tortoise discovered in 1972 by a snail biologist. George was the only tortoise on the island—and thought to be the last of his kind on Earth. Lonesome George had a "complex personality," according to his keeper of 40 years, Fausto Llerena. He visited George even on his days off. When Lonesome George died in 2012, Llerena said, "I felt I had lost my best friend."

Myrtle is the 90-year-old, 550-pound green sea turtle and undisputed queen of the Giant Ocean Tank at the New England Aquarium in Boston. Even the sharks know Myrtle's the boss; she can steal squid right out of their mouths (though her favorite food is brussels sprouts). She loves to have her shell scratched. Curious and gregarious, whenever there's a film or photo shoot in the aquarium's Giant Ocean Tank, the staff must make sure a wrangler is on the scene—just to occupy Myrtle. Otherwise, she's going to swim to where the action is and photobomb the shoot.

Poldi and Bibi were the "it couple" at the Klagenfurt Zoo in Austria—until their famous breakup. The Galápagos tortoises had lived together for 115 happy years. Then one day, for reasons only the tortoises understand, the female, Bibi, suddenly couldn't stand the sight of Poldi. Whenever he came near, she hissed at him. She bit off part of his shell. Zookeepers intervened with a trial separation. They tried romantic dinners, offering the couple delicious, special foods when they were together. Nothing worked. The two are now in separate enclosures—probably for good.

Fire Chief, a huge but gentle 42-pound snapping turtle, regained use of his paralyzed back legs thanks to his human rescuers. For most of Fire Chief's 60 to 80 years of life, he had summered in the pond behind a New England fire station. In October 2018, as he was crossing a busy road to his winter hibernation pond, he was hit by a car. His shell was smashed, his spine was broken, and his back legs and tail were paralyzed. After specialists at Turtle Rescue League repaired his shell and treated his wounds, Fire Chief began physical therapy—which included a special scooter. It was made with wheels like those designed for swivel chairs to help him exercise. Today, Fire Chief's legs and tail are working fine, and he now rules a pond of his own again!

Everyone loves baby turtles.

Even as babies, turtles look wise—and they are. By the time most turtles hatch, their moms are long gone, departing right after digging their nest, laying their eggs, and covering them with sand or soil. (There are exceptions: giant South American river turtle mothers stay nearby and call to their hatchlings to show them the way to water.) Right out of the egg, each baby turtle knows what to do: Run for cover! To the lapping waves of the ocean, the shallows of rivers and ponds, the shade of trees, rocks, or cacti, they rush for refuge. Baby turtles know they are bite-size snacks for many predators.

Leatherback Sea Turtle Hatchlings

Only 1 in 1,000 baby sea turtles, for instance, survive.

Yet turtles have endured. Thanks to the wonderful shell, their astounding talents, and their unique adaptations, turtles outlasted the dinosaurs. They survived the catastrophic meteor that hit Earth 65 million years ago.

They endured the ice age.

But they may not survive us.

Today, 61 percent of all turtle species are dangerously declining—or are already extinct in the wild.

Of all the major groups of animals with backbones—including mammals, birds, fish, and amphibians—turtles are in the worst trouble. They are slaughtered for their flesh, eggs, skin, and shells. They are sold illegally for pets and food—often at wildlife markets that can spread deadly diseases. Their homes are destroyed for human houses, stores, and roads. Climate change especially threatens sea turtles: their nesting beaches shrink as the seas rise.

Losing turtles would be a global disaster. Hawksbill sea turtles eat sponges and protect

Blanding's Turtle

coral reefs. Leatherbacks feed on jellyfish and prevent them from overpopulating the seas. Diamondback terrapins eat periwinkle snails; without turtles, the snails would turn salt marshes into barren, lifeless mudflats. Gopher tortoises construct elaborate burrows that shelter 360 other species, from armadillos to endangered frogs.

The eastern box turtle is the only known animal to disperse the seeds of the mayapple— a common woodland plant that yields chemicals that cure cancers and other diseases. The list goes on and on.

But the good news is . . .

Hawksbill Sea Turtle

You Can Help Turtles!

Protect turtles in your yard by looking before you mow the lawn. Keep your cat indoors. Don't let your dog run loose where it can injure wildlife. Avoid using pesticides.

Painted Turtle

Help turtles cross the road. Always take turtles in the direction they are headed. Never pick up a turtle by the tail—this can break its spine. To help a large snapper cross, hold the turtle by the back edge of the shell and urge it onto a large piece of cardboard or a car floor mat. Still holding the back end of the shell, drag the cardboard or floor mat, with the turtle backwards, toward the other side of the road. Turn at the end so the turtle is facing the direction it was heading. And make sure you don't get hit yourself while helping the turtle.

Shield turtle nests. Ninety percent of turtle nests are destroyed by predators like raccoons, dogs, possums, and foxes (and people dig them up too!). Some states forbid you to disturb turtle nests, even to help them, so check with local authorities—but where it's legal, you can build nest protectors at home.

Don't kidnap wild turtles.

It's against the law and it's bad for turtles. Removing just one turtle from its natural home prevents her from contributing hundreds or even thousands of baby turtles to the wild population over her long lifetime.

Common Snapping Turtle

Spotted Turtle

Never release pet turtles.

Even if your turtle looks healthy, she might transmit diseases to wild turtles. Released turtles that are not native can push out wild ones, outcompeting them for food and resources. Contact a local herpetological society to find an unwanted pet a new home.

Bring injured turtles to wildlife rehabilitators.

Even turtles with crushed shells can survive—IF they are treated promptly by trained healers. Gently place the injured turtle in a covered box with a moist towel on the bottom. Immediately call a wildlife rehabilitator— and tell them exactly where you found the turtle so it can be released back home once healed.

Eastern Painted Turtle

Volunteer.

Spend a vacation protecting sea turtle nests. Lend a hand at your local wildlife rehabilitation center. Your local aquarium, zoo, or state wildlife authority may be raising native baby turtles for release, monitoring local turtle habitats, or running a turtle hospital. Ask if you can help.

Blanding's Turtle

Avoid buying plastic,

especially single-use plastic bags (they end up in the ocean and choke sea turtles).

Green Sea Turtle

Conserve wetlands, where many

turtle species thrive. Support local and national land conservancies and laws that protect wetlands in your town and beyond.

Support turtle conservation.

Many wildlife and nature organizations help turtles and are well worth your backing! We list two of them that focus specifically on endangered turtles in the back of this book.

Ancient stories from around the world tell us how people believed the Earth was carried on the back of a turtle. Maybe that is true: wise and ancient, crucial to many ecosystems, turtles really do support the world. Stepping in to protect them gives us humans a great opportunity: it lets us take our turn to uphold the health of our planet.

Resources

- To make your yard turtle-friendly, try these tips: blog.nwf.org/2014/07/8-tips-to-protect-baby-turtles-in-your-yard
- Here's one way to build a turtle nest protector at home: turtle_tails.tripod.com/backyardturtles/byttour4.htm
- Found an injured turtle? Get the patient to a rehabilitator, fast, for the very specialized care turtles need. Here's how to find a turtle rehabilitator near you: ahnow.org; humanesociety.org/resources/how-find-wildlife-rehabilitator
- These two turtle conservation organizations focus exclusively on endangered turtles, working to protect and restore turtle populations worldwide:
  Turtle Survival Alliance: turtlesurvival.org
  Turtle Conservancy: turtleconservancy.org

Glossary

adaptation: the process of slow changes that allows a creature or species to better survive in a changing environment

ancestor: a direct relative who lived in the past. Your great-grandparents would be your ancestors, and so would your great-great-great-great-great-great-grandparents, stretching way back in time.

brackish: slightly salty water, as in a mixture of waters where river and sea meet

carapace: the hard upper shell of a turtle. The same word is sometimes used to describe the hard outer skeleton that covers a lobster, a crab, or an insect.

cloaca: an all-purpose opening for excreting digestive waste and housing reproductive organs. Present in turtles and other reptiles, birds, amphibians, and some other animals.

ecosystem: a community or group of living creatures that share and interact with one another in a particular environment

hibernation: an inactive state like deep sleep in which some animals spend the winter

keratin: a strong, protective protein that makes up human skin, hair, and nails. Keratin is also the stuff of a horse's hooves, a rhino's horn, and a turtle's shell.

plastron: the bottom shell of the turtle, which functions as a shield for its belly

rehabilitate: to restore someone to normal life after sickness or injury

terrapin: any of the different kinds of turtles that can live in slightly salty waters, where a river meets the sea

tortoise: a turtle that lives on land

turtle: any of the more than 300 different kinds of reptiles with shells, including terrapins, tortoises, and more

Bibliography

Attenborough, David. *Life in Cold Blood*. Princeton, NJ: Princeton University Press, 2008.

Bonin, Franck, Bernard Devaux, and Alain Dupré. *Turtles of the World*. Translated by Peter Pritchard. Baltimore: Johns Hopkins University Press, 2006.

Breisch, Alvin R. *The Snake and the Salamander: Reptiles and Amphibians from Maine to Virginia*. Baltimore: Johns Hopkins University Press, 2017.

Carroll, David M. *The Year of the Turtle*. Rochester, NY: Camden House Publishing, 1991.

Ernst, Carl H., and Roger W. Barbour. *Turtles of the World*. Washington, DC: Smithsonian Institution Press, 1989.

Rieppel, Olivier. *Turtles as Hopeful Monsters*. Bloomington, IN: Indiana University Press, 2017.

Steyermark, Anthony C., Michael S. Finkler, and Ronald J. Brooks, eds. *Biology of the Snapping Turtle*. Baltimore: Johns Hopkins University Press, 2008.

Matt and Sy help Turtle Survival Alliance count and weigh endangered Chinese Red-necked Pond Turtles at the TSA's Survival Center in South Carolina.

(Photo credit: Turtle Survival Alliance)